THE LITTLE
SOUP
COOKBOOK

THE LITTLE
SOUP
COOKBOOK

SMITHMARK

This edition published in 1996
by Smithmark Publishers,
a division of U.S. Media Holdings, Inc.,
16 East 32nd Street
New York, NY 10016

Smithmark books are available for bulk
purchase for sales promotion and premium
use.For details write or call the Manager of
Special Sales,
Smithmark Publishers
16 East 32nd Street
New York
NY 10016
(212) 532-6600

ISBN 0-7651-9821-5

Publisher: Joanna Lorenz
Senior Cookery Editor: Linda Fraser
Assistant Editor: Emma Brown
Designer: Patrick McLeavey
Illustrator: Anna Koska
Photographers: Michael Michaels, James Duncan, Steve Baxter,
Amanda Heywood & Michelle Garrett
Recipes: Roz Denny, Catherine Atkinson, Hilaire Walden, Annie
Nichols, Norma MacMillan, Carole Clements, Elizabeth Wolf-
Cohen, Carla Capalbo, Laura Washburn, Liz Trigg, Sarah Gates,
Sue Maggs, Jenny Stacey & Alex Barker

Printed in China
10 9 8 7 6 5 4 3 2 1

Contents

Introduction

Say soup and most people immediately conjure up an image of a steaming bowl served in a cozy kitchen on a cold winter's day. That's true as far as it goes, but soup can be so much more: a cool slither to soothe the throat, a sophisticated starter, a nourishing traveling companion, even a meal in itself.

The days when every household had a never-empty stock pot may have gone, but there's much to be said for reviving the art of making excellent stocks and soups, at least during the colder months. Home-made soup is delicious, nutritious, and inexpensive to make. Get into the habit of saving the water in which vegetables are cooked, set mushroom stalks, celery tops and parsley stalks aside, and don't wrap that leftover roast chicken in foil and leave it to languish at the back of the fridge. Instead, toss all these ingredients into a large pan, add chopped vegetables and perhaps some soaked white beans and the house will soon be filled with the satisfying aroma of simmering soup. Imagine how smug you'll feel when you serve it — and have enough for tomorrow's lunch!

Soup is so gloriously agreeable. Everyday soup — the sort you make by raiding the pantry and vegetable basket — does not demand precise quantities, nor does it need to be watched over. Most hot soups benefit from long, slow cooking, and are often even better the next day. Leftovers can be served precisely as before, or used as the basis of another soup, which may taste entirely different. Many canned or dried soups are very good, but they do tend to betray their origins; add an appropriate can or package of dried soup to a homemade soup, however, and it will be to intensify the flavor already there.

In recent years, soup has fallen from favor somewhat on the formal dinner menu. Warm salads, vegetable terrines and tiny tartlets have topped the popularity poll, with the average restaurant merely offering a single soup as an option to those demanding a wider choice. Perhaps it's time to take stock of the situation. A bowl of Borscht is every bit as beautiful as a carefully crafted salad, and a chilled avocado soup will cheer even the most jaded palate. When planning a meal for meat-eaters and vegetarians alike, start with Chilled Asparagus or Leek, Parsnip and Ginger Soup, follow with a simple main course served with an interesting salad, and all your guests will be well satisfied. And for a simple — and highly successful — party, make three or four different soups, leave them simmering over low heat, set out a selection of breads and rolls, and simply invite guests to help themselves.

Every nation has its own soups, and there are few foods that more strongly evoke a sense of place. Remember spooning up Gazpacho under a Spanish moon or marveling at the colors and flavors in a bowl of Bouillabaisse? French Onion Soup is imitated the world over, but if you've ever eaten it at midnight in Les Halles, you'll never forget the experience.

Sup your way through the soups in this collection, from classics, such as Minestrone, to the freshly innovative Melon & Basil Soup and hearty Pasta & Bean Soup — the experience is sure to bowl you over!

7

Types of Soup

BISQUE

Usually made from puréed shellfish (lobster, crab or scallops), this is a rich, creamy soup.

CHOWDER

This is the sort of soup you could make a meal of. Originally made exclusively from fish or shellfish, with bacon and vegetables (especially potatoes), it may today include other ingredients. The liquid is usually milk.

CONSOMME

A clarified soup based on meat, chicken or game stock, this owes its excellent flavor to long, slow cooking. It is always clear and may be served hot or cold and jellied.

GARBURE

A French speciality, this is a thick vegetable soup made from beans, herbs and plenty of garlic, plus a piece of preserved ham, duck, goose or turkey.

MADRILENE

A beautiful clear consommé with a deep ruby color, thanks to the addition of tomatoes. It is often served chilled and lightly jellied.

POTAGE

This is a thick soup, based on a vegetable, poultry or fish purée.

STOCK

The liquid that forms the basis of an excellent soup, made by cooking meaty bones or fish trimmings with vegetables and flavorings. Pure vegetable stock is also widely used.

VELOUTE

This is a soup enriched with cream and/or egg yolks.

Garnishes

CROUTONS

Tiny bread cubes, fried in a mixture of oil and butter (or toasted for today's fat-conscious cooks) are very popular. Try ciabatta croûtons for a change.

ALMONDS

Toasted sliced almonds are often sprinkled on top of creamy soups just before serving.

CHEESE

Grated Parmesan cheese is essential for Minestrone and similar robust soups.

BACON

Crumbled bacon is delicious on a thick bean or potato soup.

CREAM

A swirl of cream looks lovely on tomato or green pea soup. Dot the cream, then swirl with a skewer.

FILO SHREDS

Fine strips of filo pastry, drizzled with oil and baked until crisp, add color and crunch to creamy soups.

PASTA

Small pasta shapes can be used as a garnish. Add them for the final few minutes of cooking, so that they retain a bit of a bite.

HERBS

Chopped parsley or chervil is good on a clear mixed vegetable soup, while snipped chives are the classic garnish for Vichyssoise, especially when served cold.

VEGETABLE SHAPES

Carrots, celery root or rutabagas, cut into matchsticks or shaped with cookie cutters, look good in clear soups.

AVOCADO CUBES OR SLICES

An unusual garnish for a hot clear soup. Float on top

Techniques

MAKING STOCK

For rich meat stock, roast shin or marrow bones with shin or neck meat in a medium-hot oven until browned *(top left)*, then add to a large saucepan containing some thickly sliced

browned vegetables (I onion, I carrot and 2 stalks of celery). Pour in water to cover the mixture by twice its depth, then add some flavorings, such as peppercorns and a bouquet garni. Bring

the liquid slowly to a boil. Skim any scum from the surface *(right)* and simmer the stock, skimming the surface regularly, for 4–5 hours. Strain the stock *(bottom left)* and degrease it before use *(see facing page)*.

For chicken stock, cut up a meaty chicken carcass *(left)*, chop some vegetables and place in a saucepan. Cover with water, add flavorings and simmer for 2 hours. Strain *(right)*.

For fish stock, place fish trimmings (heads, skin and bones but not gills, which will give a bitter flavor) in a saucepan. Add some chopped onion and celery, with white peppercorns, parsley and some dry white wine, if desired. Cover with water *(left)*, bring to a boil and simmer, skimming from time to time, for a maximum of 40 minutes. Strain *(right)*.

For vegetable stock, chop a mixture of root vegetables (including onions [clove-studded, if desired], leeks, carrots, turnip and rutabaga) and put them in a large saucepan (*left*). Add mushroom stems, sliced celery, cabbage and parsley stalks, if you have any, and a bouquet garni. Pour in twice the depth of water or vegetable water (*right*), bring to a boil, then simmer for 1–2 hours. Strain, then season to taste.

CLARIFYING STOCK

For a jewel-like consommé, the stock must be clarified. Strain it into a clean non-aluminum pan. Whisk 2 egg whites to soft peaks; crush 2 eggshells. Add whites and shells to the soup and heat slowly, whisking until a thick white crust forms. Stop whisking, let the mixture foam up, then turn the heat off so that it falls in the pan. Repeat twice, then gently strain through a cheesecloth-lined strainer.

DEGREASING

If time permits, chill the stock or soup: the fat will solidify on top and can be easily lifted off. Alternately, you can blot the surface with paper towels.

THICKENING SOUPS

Thicken cream soups with a butter and flour paste (*beurre manié*). For every 1 cup of soup, use 1 tablespoon each flour and softened butter. Add small amounts of *beurre manié* at a time, stirring the soup well between additions.

The easiest way to thicken a vegetable soup, without adding extra fat or starch, is to scoop out some of the vegetables, purée them in a blender or food processor, and stir them back into the soup.

Oats make a very good thickener. You will need about 1 tablespoon for every 2½ cups of soup. Sprinkle over the soup about an hour before serving. Simmer, stirring occasionally.

11

Classic Soups

Cold Leek & Potato Soup

INGREDIENTS

*1 pound potatoes (about 3 large), peeled
and cubed*
6 cups chicken stock
12 ounces leeks, about 4
*⅔ cup crème fraîche or sour cream, plus
extra to garnish*
salt and freshly ground black pepper
3 tablespoons chopped fresh chives, to garnish

SERVES 6–8

1 Put the potatoes and stock in a saucepan or flameproof casserole and bring to a boil. Reduce the heat and simmer for 15–20 minutes.

2 Trim the leeks and make a slit along the length of each one with a sharp vegetable knife. Rinse them well under cold running water and then slice thinly.

3 When the potatoes are barely tender, stir in the leeks. Season with salt and pepper and simmer for 10–15 minutes, or until the vegetables are soft. Stir occasionally. If the soup appears too thick, thin it with a little stock or water.

4 Purée the soup in a food processor, or blender. If you would prefer a very smooth soup, press it through a coarse strainer. Stir in the crème fraîche, cool and then chill. To serve, ladle into chilled bowls and garnish with a swirl of crème fraîche and chopped chives.

13

Gazpacho

INGREDIENTS

½ green bell pepper, seeded and coarsely chopped
½ red bell pepper, seeded and coarsely chopped
1 medium cucumber, coarsely chopped
1 large tomato, coarsely chopped
2 scallions, chopped
Tabasco sauce (optional)
3 tablespoons chopped fresh parsley or cilantro
croûtons, to serve
SOUP BASE
1 pound ripe tomatoes, peeled, seeded,
and chopped
1 tablespoon ketchup
2 tablespoons tomato paste
¼ teaspoon sugar
¾ teaspoon salt
1 teaspoon freshly ground black pepper
5¼ cups sherry vinegar
¾ cup olive oil
1½ cups tomato juice

SERVES 4

1 To make the soup base, put the prepared tomatoes in a food processor or blender; pulse on and off until just smooth, scraping the sides of the container occasionally.

2 Add the ketchup, tomato paste, sugar, salt and pepper, sherry vinegar and oil. Pulse on and off 3–4 times, just to blend. Transfer to a large bowl. Stir in the tomato juice.

3 Put the peppers and the cucumber in the bowl of the food processor or blender and pulse on and off until they are finely chopped. Be careful not to overmix.

4 Reserve about 2 tablespoons of the chopped vegetables for the garnish and then stir the remainder into the soup base. Check the seasoning, then mix in the chopped tomato, scallions, and a dash of Tabasco sauce, if desired. Chill well.

5 To serve, ladle the chilled soup into four bowls. Sprinkle each portion with the reserved chopped vegetables, chopped fresh parsley or cilantro and a few croûtons.

14

Bouillabaisse

INGREDIENTS

3 pounds white fish, such as monkfish, silver
hake, red mullet, or bass
2 pounds oily fish, such as mackerel or eel
2 large crabs
8 lobster tails
¾ cup olive oil
2 onions, sliced
2 leeks, trimmed and sliced
2 celery sticks, sliced
1 pound tomatoes, peeled, seeded and chopped
3 garlic cloves, crushed
bouquet garni
thinly peeled strip of orange rind
2 fresh fennel sprigs
5 cups fish stock
pinch of saffron strands steeped in 2 tablespoons
boiling water
1 tablespoon tomato paste
1 tablespoon Pernod
salt and freshly ground black pepper
3 tablespoons chopped fresh parsley, to garnish
MARINADE
3 tablespoons olive oil
2 garlic cloves, finely chopped
pinch of saffron steeped in 2 tablespoons
boiling water
chopped fresh parsley, to garnish

SERVES 6

1 Discard the fins, then scale, skin and clean both the white and the oily fish. Cut the fish into chunks. Use the fish heads and tails to make the fish stock.

2 Make the marinade. Mix together the olive oil, garlic and saffron in a bowl. Pour this over the fish.

3 Leave all the shellfish in their shells. Using a cleaver, chop the crab into pieces.

4 In a large flameproof casserole, heat the oil and sauté the onions, leeks and celery until soft. Add the tomatoes, garlic, bouquet garni, orange rind and fennel. Stir in the fish stock, the saffron with its liquid and season to taste. Bring to a boil and cook for 30–40 minutes. Twenty minutes before serving, add the oily fish and shellfish and boil rapidly, uncovered, for 7 minutes. Put the white fish on top and boil for 5 more minutes. Discard the bouquet garni, orange rind and fennel sprigs.

5 Whisk the tomato paste and Pernod together and swirl it into the broth. Season to taste. Serve the bouillabaisse in heated bowls, garnished with chopped fresh parsley.

Mulligatawny Soup

INGREDIENTS

¼ cup butter or 4 tablespoons oil
2 large chicken legs, about 12 ounces each
1 onion
1 carrot
1 small turnip
1 tablespoon curry powder, to taste
4 cloves
6 black peppercorns, lightly crushed
⅓ cup lentils
3¾ cups chicken stock
¼ cup golden raisins
salt and freshly ground black pepper

SERVES 4

1 Melt the butter or heat the oil in a large saucepan, then brown the chicken over brisk heat. Transfer the chicken to a plate. Chop the onion, carrot and turnip with a sharp vegetable knife.

2 Add the chopped vegetables to the saucepan and cook them until lightly colored. Stir in the curry powder, cloves and peppercorns and cook for 1–2 minutes.

3 Add the lentils to the pan and pour in the stock. Bring to a boil, then add the golden raisins and chicken and any juices from the plate. Cover the pan and simmer gently for about 1¼ hours.

4 Take the chicken from the pan and discard the skin and bones. Chop the meat and return it to the soup to reheat. Check the seasoning before serving.

18

Borscht

INGREDIENTS

1 large cooking apple, chopped
1 onion, chopped
1 pound raw beets, peeled and chopped
2 stalks celery, chopped
½ red bell pepper, chopped
1½ cups mushrooms, chopped
2 tablespoons butter
2 tablespoons sunflower oil
8 cups chicken or vegetable stock or water
1 teaspoon cumin seeds
pinch of dried thyme
1 large bay leaf
squeeze of fresh lemon juice
salt and freshly ground black pepper
⅔ cup sour cream
fresh dill sprigs, for garnish

SERVES 6

19

1 Put the fruit and vegetables into a large pan with the butter, oil and 3 tablespoons of the stock or water. Cover and cook gently for about 15 minutes.

2 Stir in the cumin seeds and cook for 1 minute, then add the remaining stock, dried thyme, bay leaf, lemon juice and seasoning. Bring to a boil, then cover and turn down to a gentle simmer. Cook for about 30 minutes.

3 Strain the vegetables and reserve the liquid. Purée the vegetables in a food processor or blender until they are smooth and creamy. Return the vegetables to the pan, stir in the reserved liquid and reheat. Check the seasoning.

4 Serve the borscht with swirls of sour cream, garnished with a few sprigs of fresh dill.

Minestrone with Pesto Toasts

INGREDIENTS

2 tablespoons olive oil
2 garlic cloves, crushed
1 onion, halved and sliced
1 1/2 cups diced lean bacon
2 small zucchini, quartered and sliced
1/2 cup green beans, chopped
2 small carrots, diced
2 stalks celery, finely chopped
bouquet garni
1/2 cup macaroni
1/2 cup frozen peas
1 cup canned red kidney beans, drained
and rinsed
1/2 cup shredded green cabbage
4 tomatoes, peeled and seeded
salt and freshly ground black pepper
TOASTS
8 slices of Italian bread
1 tablespoon pesto
1 tablespoon grated Parmesan cheese

SERVES 4

1 Heat the olive oil in a large saucepan and gently fry the garlic and onion for 5 minutes, until just softened. Add the diced bacon, zucchini, green beans, carrots and celery to the pan and stir-fry for 3 minutes.

2 Pour 5 cups of cold water over the vegetables in the pan and add the bouquet garni. Cover the pan and simmer the soup for 25 minutes.

3 Add the macaroni, peas and kidney beans and cook for 8 minutes. Then add the cabbage and tomatoes and cook for 5 more minutes.

4 Meanwhile, make the toasts. Spread the bread slices with the pesto, sprinkle a little Parmesan over each and brown lightly under a hot grill.

5 Remove the bouquet garni from the soup, season, and serve with the pesto toasts.

COOK'S TIP
If you are making this soup for children, you could replace the macaroni with colored pasta shapes, such as shells, twists or bows.

20

French Onion Soup

INGREDIENTS

1 tablespoon butter
2 tablespoons olive oil
4 large onions, thinly sliced
2-4 garlic cloves, finely chopped
1 teaspoon sugar
½ teaspoon dried thyme
2 tablespoons flour
½ cup dry white wine
8 cups chicken or beef stock
2 tablespoons brandy (optional)
6-8 thick slices of Italian bread
1 garlic clove, peeled
*12 ounces Gruyère or Emmental
cheese, grated*

SERVES 6–8

1 In a heatproof casserole or large saucepan, heat the butter and oil. Add the onions. Cook for 10–12 minutes until they are softened and turning brown. Add the garlic, sugar and thyme. Continue cooking over medium heat for 30–35 minutes, or until the onions are well browned, stirring frequently.

2 Sprinkle all the flour over the top and stir it in until thoroughly blended. Then stir in the white wine and stock and bring the liquid to a boil. Skim off any foam that rises to the surface, then reduce the heat and simmer gently for about 45 minutes. Stir in the brandy, if using.

3 Preheat the broiler and carefully toast the slices of Italian bread on both sides. Rub each slice of the toast with the garlic clove. Place six or eight ovenproof soup bowls on a baking sheet and fill each about three-quarters full with the onion soup from the casserole.

4 Float one or two pieces of toast in each bowl. Top with the grated cheese, dividing it evenly, and broil about 6 inches from the heat for 3–4 minutes, or until the cheese begins to bubble. Serve the onion soup immediately, with its topping.

Fish & Meat
Soups

Salmon Chowder

INGREDIENTS

1 ½ tablespoons butter or margarine
1 onion, finely chopped
1 leek, finely chopped
½ cup finely chopped fennel
¼ cup flour
6 cups fish stock
2 potatoes, cut in ½-inch cubes
1 pound boneless, skinless salmon, cut into
¾-inch cubes
¾ cup milk
½ cup whipping cream
2 tablespoons chopped fresh dill
salt and freshly ground black pepper

SERVES 4

1 Melt the butter in a large saucepan. Add the onion, leek and fennel and cook over medium heat for 5–8 minutes, or until soft, stirring the mixture occasionally. Sprinkle the flour over the vegetables and stir it in. Reduce the heat to low and cook, stirring occasionally with a wooden spoon, for about 3 minutes.

2 Add the fish stock and potatoes and season with salt and pepper. Bring to a boil, then reduce the heat, cover, and simmer until all the potatoes are tender – this will take about 20 minutes.

3 Add the salmon pieces and simmer for 3–5 minutes, until they are just cooked.

4 Stir in the milk, whipping cream and dill and cook until just warmed through; do not boil. Taste and add some more salt and pepper, if needed, then serve.

Saffron Mussel Soup

INGREDIENTS

3 tablespoons unsalted butter
8 shallots, finely chopped
1 bouquet garni
1 teaspoon black peppercorns
1½ cups dry white wine
2 pounds mussels, scrubbed and debearded
2 leeks, trimmed and finely chopped
1 fennel bulb, finely chopped
1 carrot, finely chopped
several saffron strands steeped in
2 tablespoons boiling water
4 cups fish or chicken stock
2-3 tablespoons cornstarch, blended with
3 tablespoons cold water
½ cup whipping cream
1 tomato, peeled, seeded and finely chopped
2 tablespoons Pernod (optional)
salt and freshly ground black pepper
chopped fresh dill, to garnish

SERVES 4–6

1 In a large saucepan, melt half the butter over medium-high heat. Add half the shallots; cook for 1–2 minutes until softened but not colored. Add the bouquet garni, peppercorns and white wine and bring to boil. Add the mussels, cover tightly and cook over high heat for 3–5 minutes, shaking the pan occasionally, until the mussels have opened.

2 Transfer the mussels to a bowl, then strain the cooking liquid through a cheesecloth-lined strainer.

3 As the mussel shells cool down, pull them open and remove the mussels. Add any extra juices to the reserved liquid. Discard any closed mussels.

4 Rinse the pan and melt the remaining butter. Add the remaining shallots and cook for 1–2 minutes. Add the leeks, fennel, carrot and saffron and cook for 3–5 minutes, or until softened.

5 Stir in the reserved cooking liquid, bring to a boil and cook for 5 minutes until the vegetables are tender and the liquid is slightly reduced. Add the stock and bring to a boil, skimming any foam that rises to the surface. Season well and cook for another 5 minutes.

6 Stir the blended cornstarch into the soup. Simmer for 2–3 minutes, or until the soup thickens slightly, then stir in the cream, mussels and chopped tomato. Stir in the Pernod, if using, and cook for 1–2 minutes until hot. Check the seasoning and serve the soup at once, garnished with dill.

Fish Soup

INGREDIENTS

2¼ pounds mixed fish or fish pieces
(such as silver hake, red snapper or cod)
6 tablespoons olive oil, plus extra to serve
1 onion, finely chopped
1 stalk celery, chopped
1 carrot, chopped
4 tablespoons chopped fresh parsley
¾ cup white wine
3 tomatoes, peeled and chopped
2 garlic cloves, finely chopped
6 cups boiling water
salt and freshly ground black pepper
rounds of Italian bread, to serve

SERVES 6

1 Scale and clean the fish. Cut it into large pieces and rinse well in cool water.

2 Heat the oil in a large saucepan and add the onion. Cook over medium-low heat until it begins to soften. Stir in the celery and carrot, and cook for 5 minutes more. Add the parsley.

3 Add the wine, raise the heat, and cook until reduced by half. Stir in the tomatoes and the garlic, then cook for 3–4 minutes. Stir occasionally. Pour in the boiling water, and return to a boil. Cook over medium heat for 15 minutes.

4 Stir in the fish, and simmer for 10–15 minutes, or until tender. Season with salt and pepper.

5 Lift the cooked fish from the saucepan with a slotted spoon and discard any bones. Purée the fish with the soup in a blender or food processor until smooth. Taste for seasoning. If the soup is too thick, add a little more water.

6 To serve, heat the soup to simmering. Toast the rounds of Italian bread under the grill and sprinkle with olive oil. Place 2–3 rounds in each soup bowl before pouring in the hot soup.

New England Clam Chowder

INGREDIENTS

12 fresh clams, scrubbed
6 cups water
¼ cup finely diced salt pork
or lean bacon
3 onions, finely chopped
1 bay leaf
5 potatoes, peeled and diced
2 cups milk, warmed
1 cup light cream
salt and freshly ground black pepper
finely chopped fresh parsley, to garnish

SERVES 8

30

1 Rinse the clams well in cold water and drain. Place them in a deep kettle with the water and bring to a boil. Cover and steam for about 10 minutes, until the shells open. Remove from the heat.

2 When the clams have cooled slightly, remove them from their shells. Discard any clams that have not opened. Chop the clams roughly. Strain the cooking liquid through a strainer lined with cheese-cloth, and reserve it until needed.

3 In a large heavy saucepan, fry the salt pork or bacon until it renders its fat and begins to brown. Add the onions and cook over low heat for about 8–10 minutes, until softened.

4 Add the bay leaf, diced potatoes, and clam-cooking liquid to the saucepan and stir well. Bring the soup to a boil, and then cook for 5–10 minutes.

5 Stir in all the chopped clams and continue to cook until all the potatoes are tender, stirring occasionally. Add a little salt and pepper to taste.

6 Reduce the heat to low and stir in the warmed milk and cream. Simmer very gently for about 5 minutes more, then discard the bay leaf, and adjust the seasoning. Pour the soup into eight bowls and serve immediately, sprinkled with chopped fresh parsley.

Thai Chicken Soup

INGREDIENTS

1 tablespoon sunflower oil
1 garlic clove, finely chopped
2 large chicken breasts, skinned, boned and diced
½ teaspoon ground turmeric
¼ teaspoon hot chili powder
3 ounces creamed coconut
4 cups hot chicken stock
2 tablespoons fresh lime or lemon juice
2 tablespoons crunchy peanut butter
2 ounces thin egg noodles, broken into
short lengths
1 scallion, finely chopped
1 tablespoon chopped fresh cilantro
salt and freshly ground black pepper
GARNISH
2 tablespoons dried coconut
½ red chili, seeded and finely chopped

SERVES 4

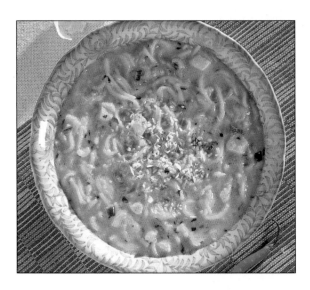

1 Heat the oil in a large saucepan. Fry the garlic until pale golden, then add the chicken and spices. Fry, stirring, for 3–4 minutes more.

2 Crumble the creamed coconut into the hot chicken stock in a jug; stir until dissolved, then add to the saucepan with the lime or lemon juice, peanut butter and egg noodles. Mix well.

3 Bring to a boil, stirring, then cover and simmer for 15 minutes. Add the scallion, cilantro, and plenty of salt and pepper. Cook for 5 minutes.

4 Meanwhile, make the garnish by browning the coconut lightly with the chili in a small ungreased frying pan. Stir the mixture constantly. Serve the soup in heated bowls, sprinkled with the browned coconut garnish.

Beef Chili Soup

INGREDIENTS

1 tablespoon oil
1 onion, chopped
¾ cup ground beef
2 garlic cloves, chopped
1 red chili, sliced
2 tablespoons flour
14-ounce can chopped tomatoes
2½ cups beef stock
15-ounce can kidney beans, drained
2 tablespoons chopped fresh parsley, plus
extra to garnish
salt and freshly ground black pepper
crusty bread, to serve

SERVES 4

1 Heat the oil in a large pan. Fry the onion and ground beef for 5 minutes, stirring frequently to break up the meat, or until browned.

2 Add the garlic cloves, red chili and flour to the pan and cook for 1 minute. Then add the tomatoes and pour in the stock. Bring the soup to a boil.

3 Stir in the drained kidney beans and season with salt and pepper to taste. Cook the soup over medium heat for another 20 minutes.

4 Add the chopped fresh parsley to the pan and check the seasoning. Pour the soup into four individual bowls and garnish with parsley. Serve with crusty bread.

Oriental Duck Consommé

INGREDIENTS

*1 duck carcass (raw or cooked), plus 2 legs or
any giblets, trimmed of as much fat as possible
1 large onion, unpeeled, with root end trimmed
2 carrots, cut into 2-inch pieces
1 parsnip, cut into 2-inch pieces
1 leek, cut into 2-inch pieces
2-4 garlic cloves, crushed
1-inch piece fresh ginger,
peeled and sliced
1 tablespoon black peppercorns
4-6 thyme sprigs or 1 teaspoon dried thyme
1 small bunch cilantro (6-8 sprigs),
leaves and stems separated*
GARNISH
*1 small carrot
1 small leek, halved lengthwise
4-6 shiitake mushrooms, thinly sliced
soy sauce
2 scallions, thinly sliced
finely shredded Napa cabbage
freshly ground black pepper*

SERVES 4

1 Put the duck, onion, carrots, parsnip, leek and garlic in a large pan or flameproof casserole. Add the ginger, peppercorns, thyme, and cilantro stems, cover with cold water and bring to a boil, skimming any foam that rises to the surface.

2 Reduce the heat and simmer for 1½–2 hours, then strain through a cheesecloth-lined strainer, discarding the bones and vegetables. Cool the duck stock and chill thoroughly. Skim any congealed fat and blot the surface carefully with paper towels.

3 Make the garnish. Cut the carrot and leek into 2-inch pieces. Thinly slice each piece lengthwise, then stack and slice into thin julienne strips. Place in a large saucepan with the mushrooms.

4 Pour in the stock and add a few dashes of soy sauce and some pepper. Bring to a boil, skimming any foam that rises to the surface. Add ground pepper to taste, then stir in the scallions and Napa cabbage. Ladle the consommé into warmed bowls and sprinkle with the cilantro leaves.

Vegetable Soups

Cream of Mushroom Soup

INGREDIENTS

1 pound Portobello mushrooms, sliced
4 ounces shiitake mushrooms, sliced
3 tablespoons sunflower oil
1 onion, chopped
1 stalk celery, chopped
5 cups vegetable stock or water
2 tablespoons soy sauce
¼ cup long-grain rice
1 ¼ cups milk
salt and freshly ground black pepper
chopped fresh parsley and sliced almonds,
to garnish

SERVES 4–6

1 Put all the mushrooms in a large saucepan with the oil, onion and celery. Heat until sizzling, then cover and simmer for about 10 minutes, shaking the pan occasionally.

2 Add the stock or water, soy sauce, rice and seasoning. Bring to a boil then cover and simmer gently for 20 minutes until the vegetables and rice are tender.

3 Strain the vegetables, reserving the stock, and purée until smooth in a food processor or blender. Return the purée and the reserved stock to the saucepan.

4 Stir in the milk, reheat until boiling and taste for seasoning. Serve the soup hot, sprinkled with a little chopped parsley and a few sliced almonds.

Provençal Vegetable Soup

INGREDIENTS

1½ cups fresh fava beans, shelled
½ teaspoon dried herbes de Provence
2 garlic cloves, finely chopped
1 tablespoon olive oil
1 onion, finely chopped
1 large leek, finely sliced
1 stalk celery, finely sliced
2 carrots, finely diced
2 small potatoes, finely diced
¾ cup green beans
5 cups water
2 small zucchini, finely chopped
3 tomatoes, peeled, seeded and finely chopped
1 cup shelled garden peas
handful of spinach leaves, cut into thin ribbons
salt and freshly ground black pepper
sprigs of fresh basil, to garnish
PISTOU
1–2 garlic cloves, finely chopped
½ cup (packed) basil leaves
4 tablespoons grated Parmesan cheese
4 tablespoons extra-virgin olive oil

SERVES 6–8

1 Make the pistou. Put the garlic, basil and cheese in a food processor or blender and process until smooth. Add the olive oil through the feed tube.

2 Place the fava beans in a pan with the herbes de Provence and 1 garlic clove. Add water to cover by 1 inch. Bring to a boil, reduce the heat and simmer for about 10 minutes until tender.

3 Heat the oil in a pan or flameproof casserole. Add the onion and leek, and cook for 5 minutes, stirring occasionally, until the onion just softens. Add the

celery, carrots and the remaining garlic clove and cook, covered, for 10 minutes, stirring occasionally.

5 Add the potatoes, green beans and water, then season lightly. Bring to a boil, skimming any foam that rises to the surface, then reduce the heat, cover and simmer gently for 10 minutes.

6 Add the zucchini, tomatoes, peas and the reserved beans and their cooking liquid. Simmer for 25–30 minutes. Add the spinach and simmer for 5 more minutes. Season, and serve, with some pistou swirled into each bowl. Garnish with basil.

Spiced Indian Cauliflower Soup

INGREDIENTS

1 large potato, peeled and diced
1 small cauliflower, chopped
1 onion, chopped
1 tablespoon sunflower oil
1 garlic clove, crushed
1 tablespoon grated fresh ginger
2 teaspoons ground turmeric
1 teaspoon cumin seeds
1 teaspoon black mustard seeds
2 teaspoons ground coriander
4 cups vegetable stock
1¼ cups plain yogurt
salt and freshly ground black pepper
fresh cilantro or parsley, to garnish

SERVES 4–6

40

1 Put the diced potato, cauliflower and onion into a large pan with the oil and 3 tablespoons of water. Heat until the water is hot and bubbling, then cover and turn down the heat. Continue cooking the mixture for about 10 minutes, stirring occasionally.

2 Add the garlic, ginger and spices. Stir well and cook for 2 minutes, stirring occasionally. Pour in the stock and season well. Bring to a boil, then cover and simmer for about 20 minutes. Stir in the yogurt, and serve garnished with fresh cilantro. Alternately, for a cold soup, chill in the fridge and add the garnish just before serving.

Italian Vegetable Soup

INGREDIENTS

3¾ cups vegetable stock
1 bay leaf
1 small carrot, cut into 2-inch-long
julienne strips
1 small leek, cut into 2-inch-long
julienne strips
1 stalk celery, cut into 2-inch-long
julienne strips
2 ounces green cabbage, finely sliced
1 cup cooked cannellini beans
¼ cup soup pasta, such as tiny shells, bows,
stars or elbows
salt and freshly ground black pepper
chopped fresh chives, to garnish

SERVES 4

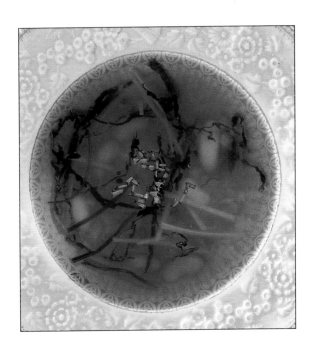

41

1 Put the stock and bay leaf into a large saucepan and bring to a boil. Add the carrot, leek and the celery, cover and simmer for 6 minutes. Add the cabbage, beans and pasta. Stir well, then simmer uncovered for about 4–5 minutes, or until all the vegetables and the pasta are tender.

2 Remove the bay leaf and season to taste. Ladle into four soup bowls and garnish with chopped chives. Serve the soup immediately.

COOK'S TIP
The success of this soup depends on the quality of the stock, so use homemade vegetable stock rather than bouillon cubes.

Leek, Parsnip & Ginger Soup

INGREDIENTS

2 tablespoons olive oil
8 ounces leeks, sliced
1 ounce fresh ginger, finely chopped
1½ pounds parsnips, roughly chopped
1¼ cups dry white wine
5 cups vegetable stock
or water
salt and freshly ground black pepper
plain yogurt and mild paprika, to garnish

SERVES 4–6

42

1 Heat the oil in a large saucepan and add the leeks and ginger. Cook gently for 2–3 minutes, until the leeks start to soften.

2 Add the chopped parsnips and cook gently for 7–8 minutes, or until softened.

3 Pour in the white wine and stock or water and bring to a boil. Reduce the heat and simmer for 20–30 minutes, or until the parsnips are tender.

4 Purée the soup in a blender or food processor. Season to taste and reheat. Serve, garnished with a swirl of yogurt and a dusting of paprika.

Broccoli & Almond Soup

INGREDIENTS

½ cup ground almonds
1 ½ pounds broccoli
1 ¼ cups skim milk
3 ¾ cups vegetable stock
salt and freshly ground black pepper

SERVES 4–6

3 Place the rest of the almonds with the broccoli, milk and vegetable stock in a blender or food processor and blend well until smooth. Season the soup to taste.

4 Reheat the soup and serve immediately, sprinkled with the reserved toasted ground almonds.

1 First, preheat the oven to 350°F and spread the ground almonds evenly on a baking sheet. Toast them for about 10 minutes, or until golden brown. Reserve a quarter of the almonds and set aside for the garnish.

2 Cut the broccoli into small florets and steam for 6–7 minutes, or until tender. Check it frequently as the broccoli must be soft but not mushy.

43

New England Spiced Pumpkin Soup

INGREDIENTS

2 tablespoons butter
1 onion, finely chopped
1 small garlic clove, crushed
1 tablespoon flour
pinch of grated nutmeg
½ teaspoon ground cinnamon
3 cups pumpkin, seeded, peeled and cubed
2½ cups chicken stock
⅔ cup orange juice
1 teaspoon brown sugar
salt and freshly ground black pepper
CROUTONS
1 tablespoon vegetable oil
2 slices of whole-grain bread without crusts,
cut into cubes
2 ounces sunflower seeds

SERVES 4

1 Heat the butter in a large saucepan, add the onion and garlic and fry gently for 4–5 minutes, or until softened. Stir in the flour, spices and pumpkin. Cover and cook gently for 6 minutes, stirring from time to time.

2 Pour in the chicken stock and the orange juice and add the brown sugar. Cover the saucepan with a lid and bring to a boil, then reduce the heat and simmer gently for about 20 minutes, or until all the pumpkin cubes have softened.

3 Pour half the mixture into a blender or food processor and process until smooth. Return the soup to the pan with the remaining chunky mixture, stirring constantly. Season and heat through.

4 Make the croûtons. Heat the vegetable oil in a frying pan and fry the bread cubes gently until they just begin to turn brown. Add all the sunflower seeds and fry for 1–2 minutes. Drain the croûtons and sunflower seeds well on paper towels.

5 Serve the soup hot with some croûtons and seeds scattered over the top. Serve the rest separately.

44

Chilled Summer Soups

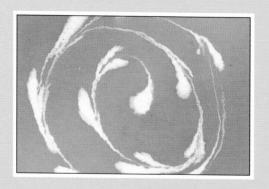

Watercress & Orange Soup

INGREDIENTS

1 large onion, chopped
1 tablespoon olive oil
2 bunches or bags of watercress
grated rind and juice of 1 large orange
2½ cups vegetable stock
⅔ cup light cream
2 teaspoons cornstarch
salt and freshly ground black pepper
a little heavy cream or yogurt, to garnish
4 orange wedges, to serve

SERVES 4

1 Soften the onion in the oil in a pan. Trim off and discard any big stalks from the watercress and add it to the pan. Cover the pan and cook the watercress for about 5 minutes.

2 Add the orange rind and juice as well as all the vegetable stock to the pan. Bring the mixture to a boil, lower the heat and cover. Simmer gently for 10–15 minutes.

3 Put the soup in a blender or food processor and process thoroughly until smooth. Strain the soup, if desired. Blend the cream with the cornstarch and add it to the soup with seasoning to taste.

4 Bring the soup gently back to a boil, stirring until it is slightly thickened. Check the seasoning and then allow the soup to cool and chill it until serving. Serve with a swirl of cream, and a wedge of orange to squeeze in at the last moment.

Green Pea & Mint Soup

INGREDIENTS

4 tablespoons butter
4 scallions, chopped
1 pound peas, fresh or frozen
2½ cups chicken or vegetable stock
2 large mint sprigs
2½ cups milk
pinch of sugar (optional)
salt and freshly ground black pepper
light cream and small mint sprigs, to garnish

SERVES 4

1 Heat the butter in a large saucepan, add the scallions, and cook gently until they are soft but not colored, stirring occasionally.

2 Stir the peas into the pan, add the stock and mint and bring to a boil. Cover and simmer very gently for 30 minutes for fresh peas or 15 minutes if you are using frozen peas, until all the peas are very tender. Remove about 3 tablespoons of the peas using a slotted spoon, and reserve for the garnish.

3 Pour the soup into a blender or food processor, add the milk and purée the soup until it is smooth. Season the soup to taste, adding a pinch of sugar, if desired. Allow the soup to cool, then cover and chill until you are ready to serve.

4 Pour the soup into bowls. Swirl a little cream into each, then garnish with mint and the reserved peas.

Chilled Fresh Tomato Soup

INGREDIENTS

*3–3½ pounds ripe tomatoes, peeled and
roughly chopped
4 garlic cloves, crushed
2 tablespoons extra-virgin olive oil (optional)
2 tablespoons balsamic vinegar
freshly ground black pepper
4 slices of whole-wheat bread, to serve
ricotta cheese and chopped toasted hazelnuts,
to garnish*

SERVES 4–6

I Place all the chopped tomatoes in a blender or food processor with the garlic and olive oil, if using. Blend well, scraping the sides, until smooth.

2 Press the tomato and garlic mixture through a strainer to remove the seeds. Stir in the balsamic vinegar. Season to taste with pepper. Place the soup in the fridge to chill.

3 Toast the bread lightly on both sides. While still hot, cut off the crusts and slice through horizontally to make two thin pieces. Gently rub off any doughy bits from the uncooked sides.

4 Cut each slice into four triangles. Place on the oven rack and toast the uncooked sides until pale golden. Watch constantly to prevent the toast from burning. Garnish each bowl of soup with a spoonful of ricotta cheese and a generous sprinkling of

chopped hazelnuts. Serve with the toast.

49

Chilled Asparagus Soup

INGREDIENTS

2 pounds fresh asparagus
4 tablespoons butter or olive oil
1½ cups sliced leeks or scallions
3 tablespoons flour
6 cups chicken stock or water
½ cup light cream or plain yogurt, plus extra to garnish
1 tablespoon finely chopped fresh tarragon or chervil
salt and freshly ground black pepper

SERVES 6

3 Heat the butter or oil in a pan. Add the leeks or scallions and cook until soft, then stir in the asparagus stalks, cover, and cook for 6–8 minutes.

4 Add the flour and stir well to blend. Cook for 3–4 minutes, uncovered, stirring occasionally.

5 Add the stock or water. Bring to a boil, stirring frequently, then reduce the heat and simmer for about 30 minutes. Season with salt and pepper.

I Cut the top 2½ inches off the asparagus. Blanch these fine tips in boiling water for 5–6 minutes, until just tender. Drain. Cut each tip into 2–3 neat pieces.

2 Trim the ends of the asparagus stalks, removing any brown or woody parts, and chop the stalks into ½-inch pieces with a sharp kitchen knife.

6 Purée the soup in a blender or food processor. If necessary, strain it to remove any coarse fibers. Stir in the asparagus tips and the cream or yogurt, and the

tarragon or chervil. Cover the bowl and chill in the fridge. Stir thoroughly before serving, and check the seasoning. Garnish each portion with a swirl of cream or yogurt.

Chilled Avocado Soup Miami

INGREDIENTS

2 large or 3 medium ripe avocados
1 tablespoon fresh lemon juice
¾ cup roughly chopped peeled cucumber
2 tablespoons dry sherry
¼ cup roughly chopped
scallions (with some of the green stems)
2 cups mild chicken stock
1 teaspoon salt
Tabasco sauce (optional)
plain yogurt or cream, to serve

SERVES 4

1 Halve, pit and peel the avocados. Chop the flesh and then process it in a blender or food processor with the lemon juice until you have a very smooth purée.

2 Add the cucumber, sherry and the scallions. Process again until smooth.

3 In a large mixing bowl, combine the avocado mixture with the chicken stock using a whisk. Beat well until thoroughly blended. Season with the salt and a few drops of the Tabasco sauce to taste, if desired. Cover the bowl with plastic wrap and chill the soup for several hours.

4 To serve, fill four individual soup bowls with the avocado soup. Place a spoonful of plain yogurt or cream in the center of each bowl and swirl carefully with a spoon to make a decorative pattern. Serve the chilled avocado soup immediately.

Melon & Basil Soup

INGREDIENTS

2 cantaloupe melons
⅓ cup superfine sugar
¾ cup water
finely grated rind and juice of 1 lime
3 tablespoons shredded fresh basil
fresh basil leaves, to garnish

SERVES 4–6

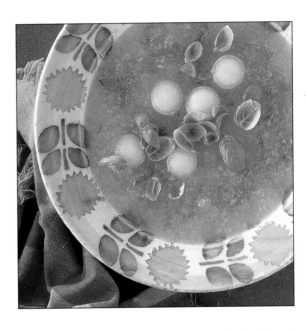

1 Cut the melons in half across the middle. Scrape out the seeds and discard. Using a melon baller, scoop out 20–24 balls and set aside for the garnish. Scoop out the remaining flesh and place it in a blender or food processor.

2 Place the sugar, water and lime rind in a small pan over low heat. Stir until dissolved then bring to a boil and simmer for 2–3 minutes. Remove from the heat and cool slightly. Pour half the mixture into the blender or food processor with the scooped-out melon flesh. Blend until smooth, adding the remaining syrup and lime juice to taste.

3 Pour the soup into a bowl, stir in the basil and chill thoroughly. Serve garnished with basil leaves and the reserved melon balls.

COOK'S TIP
Be sure to add the syrup in two stages, as the amount of sugar needed will depend on the sweetness of the melons you are using.

53

Bean, Lentil & Grain Soups

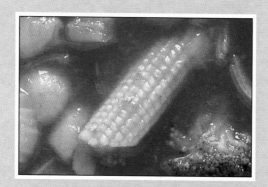

Smoked Turkey & Lentil Soup

INGREDIENTS

2 tablespoons butter
1 large carrot, chopped
1 onion, chopped
1 stalk celery, chopped
1 leek, white part only, chopped
1½ cups mushrooms, chopped
¼ cup dry white wine
5 cups chicken stock
2 teaspoons dried thyme
1 bay leaf
½ cup dried green lentils
8 ounces smoked turkey, diced
salt and freshly ground black pepper
chopped fresh parsley, to garnish (optional)

SERVES 4

1 Melt the butter in a large saucepan. Add the carrot, onion, celery, leek and mushrooms. Cook for about 3–5 minutes, until golden.

2 Stir in the wine and chicken stock. Bring to a boil and skim any foam that rises to the surface. Add the thyme and bay leaf. Lower the heat, cover, and simmer gently for 30 minutes.

3 Add the lentils, cover the saucepan and continue to cook the soup for 30–40 minutes more, until the lentils are tender. Stir the soup from time to time.

4 Stir in the diced turkey meat and season to taste with salt and pepper. Continue to cook the soup until just heated through. Ladle into four bowls and garnish with parsley, if desired.

Pasta & Bean Soup

INGREDIENTS

*scant ¾ cup dry beans (red kidney and
navy beans), soaked in cold
water overnight
1 tablespoon oil
1 onion, chopped
2 stalks celery, thinly sliced
2–3 garlic cloves, crushed
2 leeks, thinly sliced
1 vegetable stock cube
1 can or jar (14 ounces) pimientos, puréed
3–4 tablespoons tomato paste
1 cup pasta shapes
4 pieces of Italian bread
1 tablespoon pesto
1 cup baby corn, halved
½ cup each broccoli and
cauliflower florets
a few drops of Tabasco sauce, to taste
salt and freshly ground black pepper*

SERVES 4

1 Drain the beans and place in a large pan with 5 cups of water. Bring to a boil for 10 minutes, then simmer for about 1 hour, or until the beans are nearly tender.

2 When the beans are almost ready, heat the oil in a large pan and fry the vegetables for 2 minutes. Add the stock cube and the drained beans with about 2½ cups of the cooking liquid. Cover and simmer for 10 minutes, stirring occasionally.

3 Add the puréed pimientos to the pan of beans, stirring well, then stir in the tomato paste and pasta. Cook for 15 minutes. Preheat oven to 400°F.

4 Make the pesto bread. Spread the Italian bread with the pesto. Bake for 10 minutes in the preheated oven until the toasts are crisp and bubbling.

5 When the pasta is almost tender, add the corn, mixed broccoli and cauliflower florets, Tabasco sauce and salt and pepper to taste. Heat through for 2–3 minutes and serve immediately with the baked pesto-topped bread.

Split Pea Soup

Ingredients

2 tablespoons butter
1 large onion, chopped
1 large stalk celery with leaves, chopped
2 carrots, chopped
1 smoked ham hock, about 1 pound
8 cups water
1½ cups split peas
2 tablespoons chopped fresh parsley,
plus extra to garnish
½ teaspoon dried thyme
1 bay leaf
2 tablespoons lemon juice
salt and freshly ground black pepper

Serves 4–6

1 Melt the butter in a large heavy saucepan. Add the onion, celery and carrots and cook until soft, stirring occasionally.

2 Add the remaining ingredients. Bring to a boil, cover and simmer gently for 2 hours, or until the split peas are very tender.

3 Lift out the ham hock. Let it cool slightly, and then discard the skin and cut the meat from the bones. Cut the meat into small chunks.

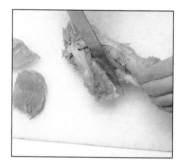

4 Return all the chunks of ham to the saucepan. Discard the bay leaf. Taste the soup and add more lemon juice, salt and pepper, if needed.

5 To serve, pour the hot soup into individual warmed soup bowls and garnish each serving with plenty of chopped fresh parsley.

58

Chicken & Chick-pea Broth

INGREDIENTS

1 roast chicken carcass
1 onion, quartered
2 stalks celery, finely chopped
1 garlic clove, crushed
a few parsley sprigs
2 bay leaves
8-ounce can chopped tomatoes
7-ounce can chick-peas
2-3 tablespoons leftover vegetables, chopped, or
1 large carrot, finely chopped
1 tablespoon chopped fresh parsley
2 slices of toast
¼ cup grated cheese
salt and freshly ground black pepper

SERVES 4

1 Pick off meat from the carcass, especially from the underside where there is often some very tasty dark meat. Set the meat aside.

2 Place the chicken carcass, broken in half, in a large saucepan with the onion, half the celery, the garlic, herbs and sufficient water to cover. Cover the pan with a lid, bring to a boil and simmer for about 30 minutes, or until you are left with about 1¼ cups of liquid.

3 Strain the stock and return it to the pan. Add the chicken, the remaining celery, the tomatoes, chick-peas (and their liquid), vegetables and parsley. Season with salt and pepper to taste and simmer for another 7–10 minutes until heated through.

4 Sprinkle the toast evenly with the cheese and grill until bubbling. Cut the toast into neat fingers or quarters and serve with, or floating on top of, the finished soup.

Pasta & Lentil Soup

INGREDIENTS

1 cup dried green or brown lentils
6 tablespoons olive oil
1/3 cup diced ham or salt pork
1 onion, finely chopped
1 stalk celery, finely chopped
1 carrot, finely chopped
8 cups chicken stock or water, or a
combination of both
1 fresh sage leaf or 3/4 teaspoon dried sage
1 fresh thyme sprig or 1/4 teaspoon
dried thyme
2 1/2 cups orzo or other
small soup pasta
salt and freshly ground black pepper
fresh cilantro or Italian parsley, to garnish

SERVES 4–6

1 Carefully sort through the lentils and remove any small stones. Place the lentils in a bowl, cover with cold water, and soak for 2–3 hours. Rinse and drain.

2 In a large saucepan, heat the olive oil and sauté the ham or pork for 2–3 minutes. Add the finely chopped onion, and cook gently until it softens.

3 Add the chopped celery and carrot. Cook for about 5 more minutes, stirring the soup frequently. Add the lentils, and stir well to coat them in the fats.

4 Pour in the chicken stock or water and add the herbs. Bring the soup to a boil. Cover with a lid and simmer over medium heat for about 1 hour or until the lentils are tender. Add salt and freshly ground black pepper to taste.

5 Stir in the pasta, and cook until it is just tender. Allow the soup to stand for a few minutes before pouring into individual heated bowls and garnishing with fresh cilantro.

Barley & Vegetable Soup

INGREDIENTS

generous 1 cup pearl barley,
preferably organic
8 cups meat stock or water, or a
combination of both
3 tablespoons olive oil
2 carrots, finely chopped
1 large onion, finely chopped
2 stalks celery, finely chopped
1 leek, thinly sliced
1 large potato, finely chopped
⅔ cup diced ham
1 bay leaf
3 tablespoons chopped fresh parsley
1 small fresh rosemary sprig
salt and freshly ground black pepper
freshly grated Parmesan cheese, to serve (optional)

SERVES 6–8

62

1 Sort through the barley, and discard any stones or other particles. Wash it in cold water. Drain, then soak the barley in cold water for at least 3 hours.

2 Drain again and place the barley in a large pan with the stock or water. Bring to a boil, lower the heat and simmer for 1 hour. Skim off any scum.

3 Stir in the oil, all the vegetables and the ham. Add the herbs. If necessary, add more water – the ingredients should be covered by at least 1 inch. Simmer for about 1–1½ hours, or until both the vegetables and the barley are very tender.

4 Taste for seasoning, adding salt and pepper if necessary. Serve the soup hot with freshly grated Parmesan cheese, if desired.

Rice & Fava Bean Soup

INGREDIENTS

2¼ pound fava beans in their pods, or
14 ounces shelled frozen fava
beans, thawed
6 tablespoons olive oil
1 onion, finely chopped
2 tomatoes, peeled and finely chopped
1 cup Arborio rice
2 tablespoons butter
4 cups boiling water
salt and freshly ground black pepper
freshly grated Parmesan cheese, to serve (optional)

SERVES 4

1 Shell the fava beans if they are fresh. Bring a large saucepan of water to a boil, and blanch the beans, fresh or frozen, for 3–4 minutes, then rinse them thor-  oughly under cold running water, and pop off the skins between your index finger and thumb.

2 Heat the oil in a large saucepan. Add the onion. Cook over low to medium heat until it softens. Stir in the beans, and cook them gently for about 5 minutes, stirring often to coat them with the oil. Season with salt and pepper. Add the tomatoes, and cook for 5 more minutes, stirring often.

3 Stir in the rice. After 1–2 minutes add the butter, and stir until it melts. Pour in the boiling water, a little at a time, until the whole amount has been added. Taste  for seasoning. Continue cooking the soup until the rice is tender. Serve hot, with freshly grated Parmesan cheese, if desired.

63

Index